ELISSA THOMPSON

DRAWING
NEW YORK'S
SIGHTS AND SYMBOLS

Enslow Publishing

101 W. 23rd Street
Suite 240
New York, NY 10011
USA

enslow.com

Published in 2019 by Enslow Publishing, LLC.
101 W. 23rd Street, Suite 240, New York, NY 10011

Library of Congress Cataloging-in-Publication Data
Names: Thompson, Elissa, author.
Title: Drawing New York's sights and symbols / Elissa Thompson.
Description: New York : Enslow Publishing, 2019. | Series: Drawing our states
| Includes bibliographical references and index. | Audience: Grades 2-5.
Identifiers: LCCN 2018008782| ISBN 9781978503212 (library bound) | ISBN
9781978504844 (pbk.) | ISBN 9781978504851 (6 pack)
Subjects: LCSH: New York (State)—In art—Juvenile literature. | Emblems in
art—Juvenile literature. | Drawing—Technique—Juvenile literature.
Classification: LCC NC825.N49 T49 2019 | DDC 741.09747—dc23
LC record available at https://lccn.loc.gov/2018008782

Printed in the United States of America

To Our Readers: We have done our best to make sure all websites in this book
were active and appropriate when we went to press. However, the author and
the publisher have no control over and assume no liability for the material
available on those websites or on any websites they may link to. Any comments
or suggestions can be sent by email to customerservice@enslow.com.

Photo Credits: Cover and p. 1 inset illustration and interior
pages instructional illustrations by Laura Murawski.

Cover, p. 1 atsurkan/Shutterstock.com (photo); p. 6 TTstudio/Shutterstock.
com; p. 8 Three Lions/Hulton Archive/Getty Images; p. 9 Fine Art/Corbis
Historical/Getty Images; p. 10 Schwabenblitz/Shutterstock.com; p. 12
BigAlBaloo/Shutterstock.com; p. 14 corund/Shutterstock.com; p. 16 Kuzmenko
Viktoria photografer/Shutterstock.com; p. 18 Marc Bruxelle/Shutterstock.
com; p. 20 FotoRequest/Shutterstock.com; p. 22 Skreidzeleu/Shutterstock.
com; p. 24 Jam Norasett/Shutterstock.com; p. 26 Education Images/Universal
Images Group/Getty Images; p. 28 Sean Pavone/Shutterstock.com.

CONTENTS

WORDS TO KNOW

American Revolution Battles that soldiers from the colonies fought against England for freedom.

coat of arms A design on and around a shield or on a drawing of a shield.

flanks The areas between the lower ribs and the hip on either side of the body.

French and Indian War The battles fought between 1754 and 1763 by England, France, and Native American allies for control of North America.

glaciers Large masses of ice in very cold regions or on the tops of high mountains.

motto A short sentence or phrase that says what someone believes or what something stands for.

Phrygian Of or related to Phrygia, an ancient extinct area in Indo-Europe.

WELCOME TO NEW YORK

New York was the eleventh state to join the United States in 1778, but it had a very rich history long before then. Native Americans settled in what is now New York more than five thousand years ago! Today more than nineteen million people call New York home, and it is the fourth most populated state in the country. New York City is the most populated city in the state—and the entire country. More than eight million people live there.

New York is a hub for arts, agriculture, and business. There are many museums and galleries, performing arts centers, and theaters in the state. New York also has about thirty-six thousand farms. Dairy farming is big business in New York. You can find dairy farms in the Hudson, the St. Lawrence, and the Mohawk valleys. New York is also home to many apple farms. Exciting sights in New York include Niagara Falls, the Empire State Building, and the Baseball Hall of Fame in Cooperstown.

New York's most famous city is New York City. "The City that Never Sleeps" always has something exciting going on. There's Central Park with an ice skating rink and zoo; Broadway, where

The famous New York City skyline greets more than sixty million visitors from around the world each year.

many talented actors perform in plays and musicals; and the United Nations, an international organization of countries devoted to world peace. Most major book and magazine publishers have offices in New York City, as do television and radio stations. Financial companies also call the city home.

In 1624, the Dutch settled New York. In 1664, King Charles II of England took over the region. He gave it to his brother James, the duke of York and Albany, in England. The cities of New York and Albany are named for him.

The state got its nickname, the Empire State, when George Washington predicted it would be the center of a new empire. George Washington's inauguration as the nation's first president took place in New York City on April 30, 1789.

This book will give you a chance to draw some of New York's sights and symbols. In each chapter, you will find step-by-step instructions explaining how to draw that chapter's subject. The drawing shapes and terms below can help you, too.

You will need the following supplies to draw New York's sights and symbols:

- A sketch pad
- An eraser
- A number 2 pencil
- A pencil sharpener

These are some of the shapes and drawing terms you need to know to draw New York's sights and symbols:

- Shading
- Squiggle
- Teardrop
- Vertical line
- Wavy line
- 3-D box
- Almond shape
- Horizontal line
- Oval
- Rectangle

MEET EDWARD HOPPER

Edward Hopper was an important painter known for his realist style, which means he painted recognizable scenes from ordinary life.

Hopper was born in 1882 in Nyack, New York. His family supported his dream of becoming an artist, and he studied art in New York City in the early 1900s. He traveled to Europe several times and eventually moved to the Greenwich Village neighborhood of New York City, where he kept an art studio for the rest of his life.

Hopper painted many of his works in a small New York City apartment.

Hopper married artist Josephine Verstille Nivison, a fellow student in one of his art classes, in 1923. Jo, as he called her, helped with his art. She posed as the woman in almost all of his paintings, organized his studio, and kept track of all of his art sales.

At Hopper's first solo show in 1920, with only his paintings on display, no one bought any of his art. But soon his art became more popular. He had another art show where every painting sold! His painting *House by the Railroad* was one of the first to be purchased for New York City's new Museum of Modern Art in 1930.

Many say Hopper's most famous painting is *Nighthawks*, which shows three people and a waiter at a diner at night. They are sitting apart and not talking, which showcases the loneliness people felt during the 1940s and World War II.

Hopper remains a very popular artist, even after his death in 1967. Many people still love to look at his paintings, like *New York Movie*, which shows a movie usher lost in her own daydreams.

Hopper painted *Nighthawks* in 1942. The red-headed woman pictured was modeled by his wife, Jo.

States, Bodies of Water, and Another Country: New York's Borders

To the north of New York is another country: Canada! The Canadian provinces of Ontario and Quebec border New York's northern edge. New York is also bordered by five states. To the southwest is Pennsylvania. New

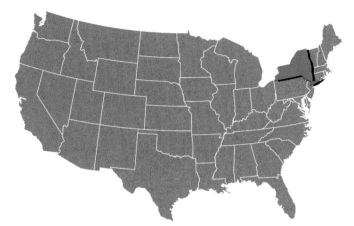

Jersey lies to the south. To the east are Vermont, Massachusetts, and Connecticut. New York also borders three large bodies of water. Lake Ontario and Lake Erie are northwest and west of the state. The Atlantic Ocean lies to the southeast. New York has four mountain ranges: the Adirondack, the Catskill, the Shawangunk, and the Taconic Ranges.

1

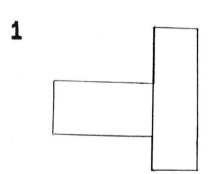

Start by drawing two rectangles.

2

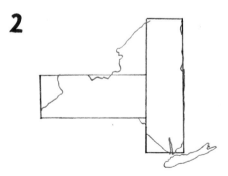

Using the rectangles as guides, draw the shape of New York.

3

Erase extra lines. Draw a circle for New York City and a square for Allegheny State Park.

4

Draw in the Hudson River, and add upside-down V's for the Catskill Mountains.

5

To finish your map, draw a star to mark Albany, the capital of New York.

Albany

New York City

Allegheny State Park

Hudson River

Catskill Mountains

6

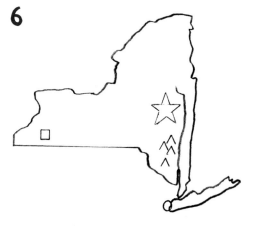

Erase extra lines in the star. Draw a key in the upper right corner to mark New York's points of interest.

Ladies Liberty and Justice: The Great Seal of New York

New York's state seal changed five times between 1777 and 1882. The seal has the state's coat of arms in a circle with the words "The Great Seal of the State of New York." Two women hold a shield. On the left is the goddess Liberty, who stands for freedom. On the right is the goddess Justice, who stands for equal treatment for everyone under the law. The state's motto, "Excelsior," which means "ever upward," is at the bottom. There is a sun rising over the cliffs near West Point while below ships sail on the Hudson River. On top is a globe and an eagle.

1

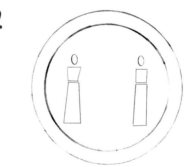

Start by drawing two large circles for the seal background. Add two ovals for the goddesses' heads.

2

Draw four, four-sided shapes as shown to outline the goddesses' bodies.

3

Draw clothing and shoes as shown. Add the goddesses' arms and necks.

4

Erase extra lines. Draw a pole with a cap on top of it in Liberty's hand. Draw a sword, a scale, and a sash for Justice.

5

Draw a face and hair on each goddess. Justice, on the right, is wearing a blindfold.

6

Add the words "THE GREAT SEAL OF THE STATE OF NEW YORK." Add a ribbon at the bottom with the word "EXCELSIOR." To learn how to draw the details of the shield, refer to the New York state flag drawing instructions on page 15.

Revolutionary Roots: The State Flag

The state flag New York has now is based off the flag it had during the Revolutionary War. It became the state's official flag in 1901. Like the state seal, the flag has the state's coat of arms. The goddess Liberty is holding a pole topped with a liberty cap, or a Phrygian cap. In ancient Rome, a freed slave was given a Phrygian cap to symbolize his or her freedom. The goddess Justice is blind-folded because she sees no difference between people and treats everyone fairly.

1

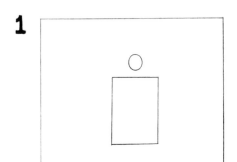

Draw a large rectangle for the flag's field and a small rectangle in the center for the shield. Add a circle for the globe.

2

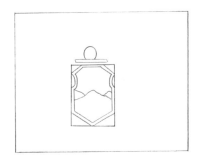

Using the rectangle as a guide, draw the shield in the center and the mountains inside the shield. Add a thin rectangle underneath the globe.

3

Erase extra lines. Add two circles for the eagle's body and two triangles for its wings.

4

Draw in the shape of the eagle. Add a circle in the shield for the sun. Draw a shoreline at the front of the shield using wavy lines.

5

Erase extra lines. Add rectangles and triangles for the ships in the center. Add wavy lines for water behind the ships.

6

Erase extra lines. To learn how to draw the goddesses on the flag, refer to the New York state seal drawing instructions on page 12.

Put It to a Vote: The Rose

In 1890, schoolchildren in New York voted for a state flower. They chose between the goldenrod and the rose. The rose won, even when there was another vote in 1891. The rose wasn't made the official state flower until April 20, 1955. Roses come in many different colors, including red, orange, yellow, pink, and white. Roses can be from 0.5 to 7 inches (1 to 18 centimeters) wide. Most wild roses usually have five petals and sharp thorns. Cultivated roses often have multiple sets of petals.

1

Draw a circle for the center of the rose. Add curved shapes around the center as shown.

2

Add four rounded V shapes for petals.

3

Add eight more petal shapes as shown.

4

Now add another layer of petals.

5

Erase extra lines. Add a stem and leaves.

6

Add shading and detail to your rose.

A Sweet Tree: The Sugar Maple

In 1956, New York named the sugar maple its official state tree. Sugar maples have short trunks and many leaf-covered branches. The sugar maple usually grows to be from 60 to 75 feet (18 to 23 meters) tall. The bark of a sugar maple is dark brown and grooved. In the fall, the maple's five-pointed leaves change color to bright reds, oranges, and yellows. Sugar maple trees have liquid inside them called sap. Syrup makers use special tools to drill into the maple's trunk to get the sap. The sap is then made into maple syrup.

1

Begin by drawing a tall trunk that comes to a point. You can use wiggly lines so that the trunk has the look of bark.

2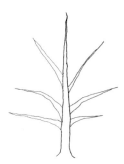

Now add six large branches. They come out of the trunk like pointy fingers.

3

Add thinner branches by drawing wiggly lines.

4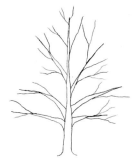

Add even smaller branches to the tree.

5

Now draw the outline of the leafy top of the tree around all of the branches.

6

Shade the trunk of the tree using long, dark lines. Begin filling in the leaves. You can create the leaves by using a squiggly line. Let your hand shake as you are drawing. Make some areas darker to create shadows.

Blue, Red, and White: The Eastern Bluebird

In 1970, New York chose the eastern bluebird as its official state bird. Male eastern bluebirds have different coloring than female eastern bluebirds. The heads, tails, backs, and wings of the males are bright blue. Their sides, flanks, and throats are chestnut red, and their bellies are white. The females have gray-blue heads, dull brown backs, and blue tails and wings. Bluebirds build their nests in dead trees or wooden fence posts. They will even use nest boxes people leave for them.

1

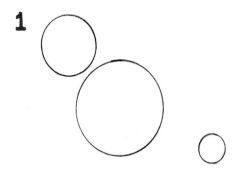

Start by drawing three circles for the rough shape of the eastern bluebird.

2

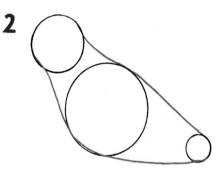

Connect your circles to form the shape of the bird's body.

3

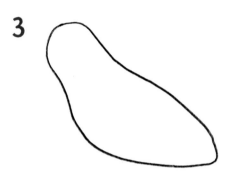

Erase extra lines and smudges.

4

Add one triangle for the beak, one for the tail, and one for the wing.

5

Erase extra lines. Round out the shape of the bird's wing. Draw the legs, the feet, and an eye.

6

Add shading and detail to your bluebird. You can also smudge your lines to make the shading look more natural.

Monument to Friendship: The Statue of Liberty

The Statue of Liberty is one of the tallest statues in the entire world! It is 151 feet (46 m) tall. There are 354 steps to climb to reach the crown and 192 steps to reach the top of the pedestal. The Statue of Liberty stands on Liberty Island in New York Harbor. It was a gift from France to America to celebrate the friendship between the countries. The statue was designed by French sculptor Frédéric-Auguste Bartholdi. It was dedicated in 1886 by US president Grover Cleveland.

1

Draw an oval for the statue's head. Add the four-sided shape shown for her body. Add a rectangle for the book she holds.

2

Form two rectangles for the statue's pedestal. Add another rectangle for her right arm.

3

Draw the shape of the statue's arm and hand. Add a rectangle and the flame shape for the torch she carries.

4

Erase extra lines. Draw the statue's left hand and her robe.

5

Erase extra lines. Draw the statue's crown as shown. Add details to her face.

6

Add shading and detail to your picture.

Majestic Wonder: Niagara Falls

Niagara Falls is made up of two waterfalls in two different countries, the United States and Canada. Both located on the Niagara River, the American Falls is in New York and is 176 feet (54 m) high and 1,060 feet (323 m) across. Horseshoe Falls is on the Canadian side and is 167 feet (51 m) high and 2,200 feet (670.5 m) across. Niagara Falls was created about twelve thousand years ago, when melting ice from large glaciers created the Niagara River. After many years, the river cut through a high cliff, creating Niagara Falls.

1

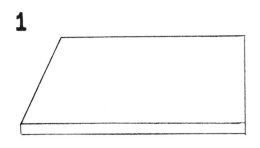

Start by forming two slanted rectangles for the viewing area.

2

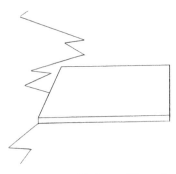

Erase extra lines. Add slanted lines for the shape of the falls.

3

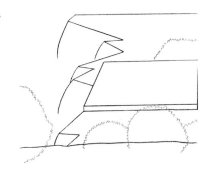

Add curved lines for the falling water. Add a line at the top and at the side for the far edge of the falls.

4

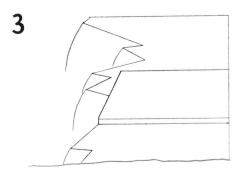

Add shrubs using little M shapes.

5

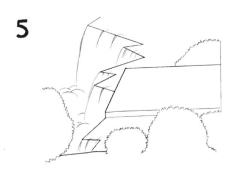

Erase extra lines. Add small half circles for the bottom of the falls. Add more lines for the water.

6

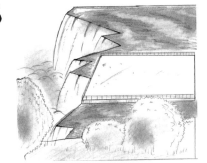

Add shading and detail. Great job!

Living History: Fort Ticonderoga

In 1755, the French built Fort Carillon on the western shore of Lake Champlain. During the French and Indian War (1754–1763), the British captured the fort and renamed it Ticonderoga. "Ticonderoga" means "land between two waters" in the Iroquois language. During the American Revolution, in 1775, patriot Ethan Allen and his men captured the fort. The British retook the fort in 1777, abandoning it in 1780. In 1790, New York took control of what was left of the fort. In 1908, the fort was restored. It is now a museum you can visit.

1

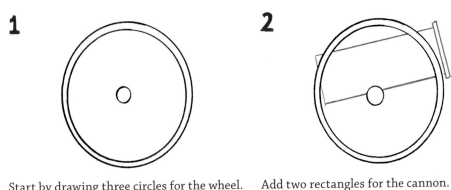

Start by drawing three circles for the wheel.

2

Add two rectangles for the cannon.

3

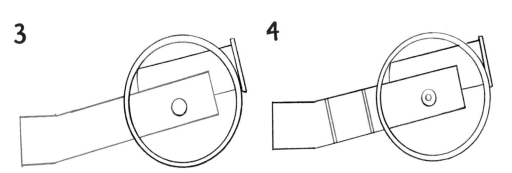

Add the shape shown to form the cannon's support. Erase extra lines.

4

Draw another circle in the center of the wheel. Add two thin rectangles on the cannon's brace.

5

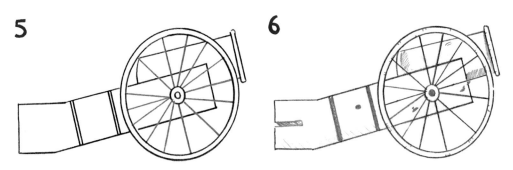

Erase extra lines. Add 14 lines for the spokes in the wheel.

6

Add detail to your cannon.

A $25 Million Building: New York's Capitol

New York's state capitol building in Albany cost $25 million and took from 1867 to 1899 to build! The capitol is 400 feet (122 m) long and 300 feet (91 m) wide. The building's first designer, British architect Thomas Fuller, was replaced by American architects Leopold Eidlitz and Henry Hobson Richardson. The Great Western Staircase, also called the Million Dollar Staircase, took fourteen years and more than $1 million to build. It has 444 steps and is 119 feet (36 m) high.

1

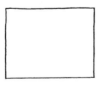

First draw a rectangle.

2

Inside the rectangle, draw a square. Notice that the square is toward the bottom center of the rectangle.

3

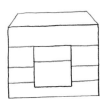

For the roof, draw two slanted vertical lines and one horizontal line. Now draw the horizontal lines inside the rectangle and another one inside the square.

4

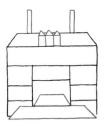

Now draw the outline of the two-level staircase. Use the same shape you used for the roof. Draw two chimneys on top of the roof. Draw three rectangles in the center of the roof. Now add three triangles on top of the rectangles.

5

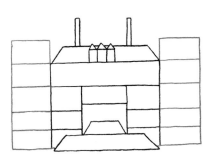

For the wings of the building, draw two rectangles. Add horizontal lines inside them.

6

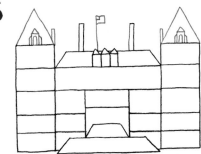

Add a triangle to the top of each wing. Add details inside the triangles as shown. Draw two more thin chimneys next to the pointed triangles. Now add the flag.

7

Now you are ready to add all of the arched and square windows. They are all in groups of three.

8

To finish your drawing, add detail and shading.

FACTS ABOUT NEW YORK

Statehood • July 26, 1788, 11th state

Area • 47,224 square miles (122,309.5 square kilometers)

Population • 18,196,600

Capital • Albany, population, 100,000

Most Populated City • New York City, population, 7,322,600

Industries • Printing and publishing, scientific instruments, electrical equipment, machinery, chemical products, tourism

Agriculture • Apples, dairy products, poultry and eggs, nursery stock, cherries, cabbage, and corn

Animal • Beaver

Song • "I Love New York"

Bird • Eastern bluebird

Flower • Rose

Freshwater Fish • Brook trout

Tree • Sugar maple

Gemstone • Garnet

Insect • Ladybug

Shell • Bay scallop

Fruit • Apple

Motto • Excelsior, "Ever Upward"

Nickname • The Empire State

LEARN MORE

Books

Crane, Cody. *New York*. New York, NY: Scholastic, 2018.

Malam, John. *You Wouldn't Want to be a Worker on the Statue of Liberty!* New York, NY: Scholastic, 2017.

Stine, Megan. *Where Is the Brooklyn Bridge?* New York, NY: Grosset & Dunlop, 2016.

Websites

New York Philharmonic

http://www.nyphilkids.org

Play games, learn about composers and instruments, and meet the conductors of this famous New York–based orchestra, the oldest in the United States.

New York Public Library: Kids

kids.nypl.org

Visit the amazing New York Public Library right from the Internet! Cool games and ebooks will help you learn all about the world.

New York State: Department of State: Kid's Room

dos.ny.gov/kids_room

Learn all about what makes New York State great, including fun facts, the history of governors, and more.

INDEX